ENGINEERING THE HUMAN BODY

EXTRA SENSES

by Tammy Gagne

FOCUS
READERS

NAVIGATOR

WWW.FOCUSREADERS.COM

Focus Readers is distributed by North Star Editions:
sales@northstareditions.com | 888-417-0195

Produced for Focus Readers by Red Line Editorial.

Content Consultant: Ella Striem-Amit, Assistant Professor of Neuroscience, Georgetown University

Photographs ©: GarryKillian/Shutterstock Images, cover, 1; Burger/Phanie/Science Source, 4–5; alle12/iStockphoto, 7; Glen Chapman/AFP/Getty Images, 8, 24–25; Red Line Editorial, 11; Svitlana Bezuhlova/Shutterstock Images, 12–13; Andrey_Popov/Shutterstock Images, 15; Philippe Psaila/Science Source, 17, 21; Peter Svensson/AP Images, 18–19; SeventyFour/iStockphoto, 23; alexialex/Shutterstock Images, 27; LightField Studios/Shutterstock Images, 29

Library of Congress Cataloging-in-Publication Data
Names: Gagne, Tammy, author.
Title: Extra senses / by Tammy Gagne.
Description: Lake Elmo, MN : Focus Readers, [2020] | Series: Engineering the
  human body | Audience: Grades 4 to 6. | Includes bibliographical
  references and index.
Identifiers: LCCN 2019006352 (print) | LCCN 2019008813 (ebook) | ISBN
  9781641859714 (pdf) | ISBN 9781641859028 (ebook) | ISBN 9781641857642
  (hardcover) | ISBN 9781641858335 (pbk.)
Subjects: LCSH: Senses and sensation--Technological innovations--Juvenile
  literature. | Neurophysiology--Technological innovations--Juvenile
  literature.
Classification: LCC QP434 (ebook) | LCC QP434 .G34 2020 (print) | DDC
  612.8--dc23
LC record available at https://lccn.loc.gov/2019006352

Printed in the United States of America
Mankato, MN
May, 2019

ABOUT THE AUTHOR

Tammy Gagne has written more than 200 books for both adults and children. She resides in northern New England with her husband and son. Her most recent titles include *Artificial Organs* and *Exoskeletons*.

TABLE OF CONTENTS

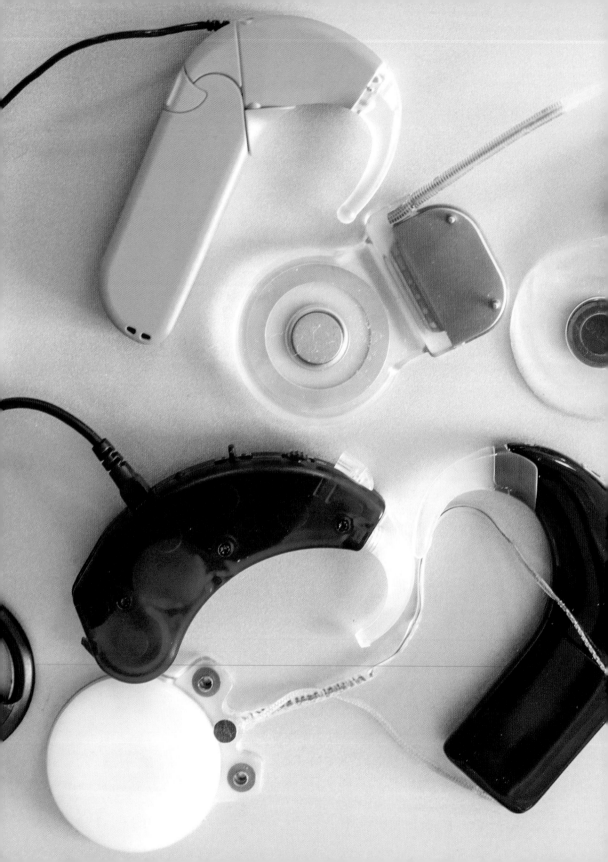

CHAPTER 1

SENSORY PERCEPTION

Jonathan Leach was born completely deaf. Hearing aids couldn't help with his hearing loss. Sign language only helped him communicate with certain people. A cochlear **implant** could help him hear. But this device is most useful when it is placed early in life. As an adult, Leach helped scientists test a new device.

Cochlear implants are placed under the skin by a surgeon.

The technology would help him **perceive** sound without using his ears.

Humans experience the world through five natural senses. These senses are sight, hearing, smell, touch, and taste. If one sense is not working, another sense can sometimes stand in for it.

Engineers used this idea to create a vest. The vest would **vibrate** when it sensed sounds. It would allow Leach to **interpret** sounds through his sense of touch. The vibrations would take the place of his hearing.

To test the vest, Leach sat in front of a whiteboard. Another person spoke to him. Leach couldn't hear the person's words.

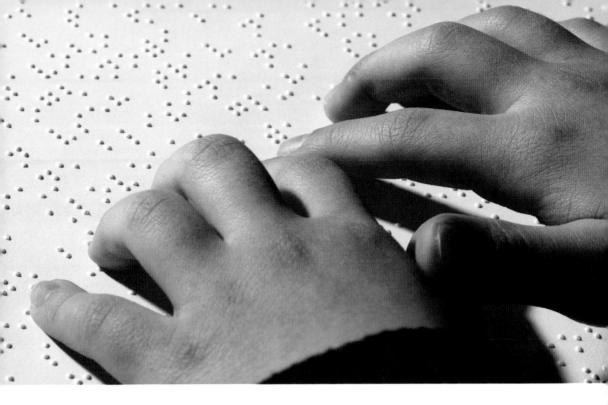

Though they cannot see words, blind people can learn to read braille through their sense of touch.

But his vest picked up the sound waves. The vest vibrated. By interpreting the vibrations, Leach was able to write each word on the board. The vest gave him an extra sense to replace his hearing.

The technology is still limited. Cochlear implants could achieve the same results.

The vest Jonathan Leach tested can change spoken words or other information into vibrations that the user can feel.

But the technology can be improved. Leach's test showed the possibilities of working with extra senses.

Extra senses help people perceive information that their natural senses cannot. In some cases, extra senses can replace natural senses. In other cases, they can give someone an additional sense. Natural senses perceive only a small part of the world. For example, human eyes cannot see **ultraviolet light**. Scientists are developing extra senses that would allow humans to perceive this information.

INSPIRED BY ANIMALS

Many animals have senses that humans do not. For example, bats use a sense called echolocation. A bat makes a sound. The sound bounces off objects and creates echoes. The echoes then return to the bat's ears. The bat interprets the echoes. It can tell where the objects are. Echolocation helps the bat find food in the dark. This sense can also help some blind people move through the world. They click their tongues and listen. They learn where objects are.

SENSORY SUBSTITUTION

Using one sense to stand in for another is called sensory substitution. For example, Jonathan Leach's vest substitutes touch for hearing. A microphone on the vest picks up sound waves. It sends signals to small motors in the vest. These motors vibrate in reaction to the signals. Different signals result in different patterns of vibrations.

The user feels the vibrations through the sense of touch. Over time, the user's brain connects vibration patterns with letters and words. The user does not hear the sounds. Instead, the user's brain understands the "language" of the vest.

Training with the vest takes several days. During this time, the user's brain learns an entire vocabulary based on vibrations. After several

This vest turns sound into data for the user's brain. With the help of a microphone, the vest sends sound waves to tiny motors within the clothing. These motors rely on the user's sense of touch to communicate with the user's brain.

MICROPHONE

MOTORS

months, the deaf person can easily understand many spoken words.

CHAPTER 2

WHY EXTRA SENSES?

Natural senses work because humans have sense **organs**. These organs include the eyes, ears, skin, nose, and tongue. These organs take in information from the world. This information includes light waves, sound waves, pressure, and more. The organs send signals to the brain. The brain interprets these signals.

People with natural vision can see things because light waves bounce off objects and hit their eyes.

The person sees, hears, feels, smells, or tastes something.

People sometimes lose one of their senses. Their sense organ no longer works. They have to find ways to live without the lost sense. For example, blind people might use canes or guide dogs as they move around. Extra-sense devices could also help. The devices could send information to the brain. The user's brain could learn to interpret the information.

Scientists used to think the brain could not change. They believed it worked a certain way and could not grow. But then scientists discovered brain **plasticity**. They learned that the brain can change

A blind person might tap a support cane on the ground in order to move around safely.

based on a person's experiences. The brain can learn to work in new ways.

Scientist Paul Bach-y-Rita used this idea to explore sensory substitution. In 1969, he developed a device to substitute touch for sight. Blind users wore a set of small plates on their backs.

They also held a camera. The camera took in visual information. The plates vibrated in response to those visuals. Users' brains learned to interpret those vibrations as images. Their working senses replaced the sense that was not working.

Over time, Bach-y-Rita improved his device. His company made the BrainPort. This device sits on the user's tongue and is connected to a camera. The camera takes an ongoing video of the user's surroundings. The device responds to the video by pricking the user's tongue. The user's tongue sends signals to the brain. The brain learns to interpret these signals as images. Blind users can make their way

This camera takes in information and sends it to a pad on the user's tongue or lower back in the form of vibrations.

through obstacle courses. They can throw balls into baskets.

Other scientists are developing devices to help blind people, too. The technology is improving. Over time, more people will benefit from extra senses.

CHAPTER 3

EXTRA SENSES TODAY

Today's extra senses come in different forms. Some extra senses do not replace a person's natural senses. For example, people can wear night vision goggles to see infrared light. This form of light is made up of heat waves. People cannot see infrared light with their eyes. But they can with these goggles.

Some phone cameras can take infrared images. Warm objects appear bright on the screen.

Wearers see the heat given off by bodies and other objects.

Other extra senses use sensory substitution. They replace a natural sense that is not working. Examples include the BrainPort and Jonathan Leach's vest. These devices are often wearable. Many substitute the missing sense with touch.

PORTABLE SENSES

To be most helpful, an extra-sense device must be easy to take from one place to another. People don't want to carry heavy machines with them. For this reason, engineers try to make devices that are wearable. A device that can be worn as clothing does not interfere with a person's everyday life.

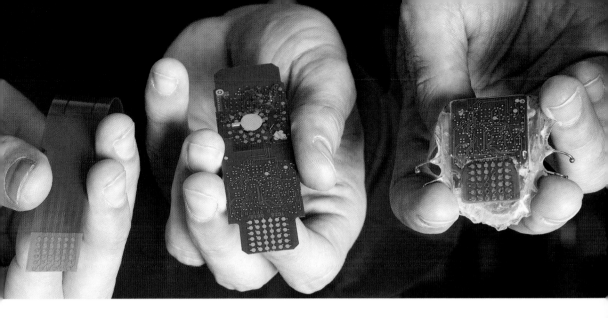

These devices are similar to the BrainPort. They are worn in the mouth and can substitute touch for sight.

Some extra senses send information using implants. They connect directly to a person's **nerves**. They send signals to the brain. They do the work of a damaged sense organ. One example is the cochlear implant. It helps deaf people hear.

Another example is smart skin. People who lose an arm or a leg can receive an **artificial** limb that they can move.

But the limb does not have the sense of touch. Scientists have created an artificial hand with smart skin. It allows the user to perceive touch in a new way.

Smart skin senses information about the hardness or softness of objects. It sends that information to a computer. The computer changes that information into signals the brain will understand. Then the computer sends these signals to implants in the user's upper arm. These implants connect to the user's nerves. The nerves send the signals to the brain. The brain interprets the signals as touch.

Finally, some extra senses affect the brain directly. These devices are brain

Artificial legs restore movement to their users. But most of today's models do not restore the sense of touch.

implants. Scientists have developed one device that detects infrared light. They have tested it on rats. The rats learned to see infrared light within four days. A similar implant could let humans see heat.

CHAPTER 4

THE FUTURE OF EXTRA SENSES

Many extra senses work to replace a person's lost sense. But scientists are also trying to develop entirely new senses. This technology could transform the way the world works.

One example is a vest that would help users sense weather patterns. The vest could help hikers make safe decisions.

Scientist David Eagleman developed a vest that can train users' brains to sense new information.

The vest would work because human brains can learn to make sense of complex information. The vest would turn weather information into vibrations. Users' brains could learn to identify which patterns of vibrations mean good weather and which mean bad weather. Users could decide when it is safer to keep hiking or to turn back.

Another example is a vest that would be programmed to monitor vital signs. These health signs include heart rate and blood pressure. The vest could give users a better understanding of their health. Sensing this information could alert users to problems before they become serious.

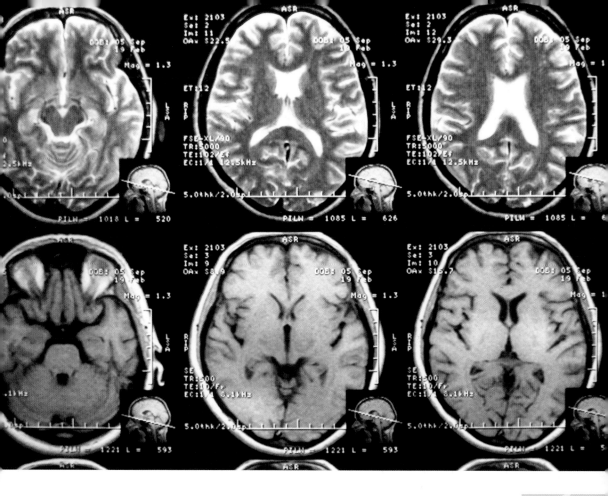

Researchers study brain scans to see how the human brain responds to new sense information.

Another device could give humans 360-degree vision. People with normal sight can see objects that are directly in front of them or to their sides. But they cannot see objects that are behind them.

An extra sense could make this feat possible. Life could be safer with 360-degree vision. For example, people might have fewer car accidents if they could see in all directions.

The ways in which extra senses could benefit humankind are limitless. As

LIMITLESS POSSIBILITIES

In the future, people will likely have access to many extra senses. The possibilities are limitless. For example, scientists are making devices that substitute sound for sight. Companies are creating devices that alert users when they are facing north. People are implanting magnets into their fingers. The magnets let them feel Earth's magnetic field.

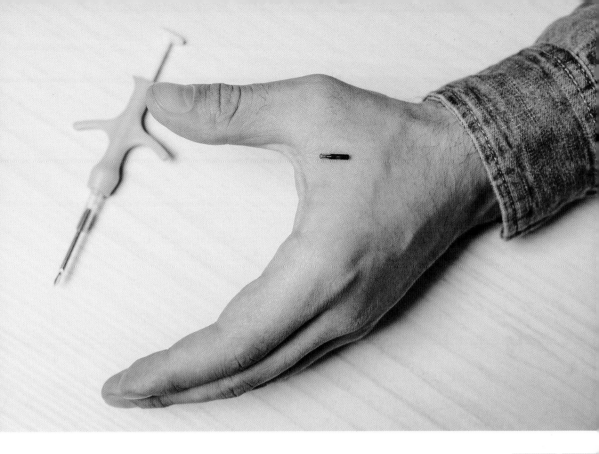

Some people are getting microchip implants. These tiny implants will change how people interact with the world.

technology develops, engineers will create even more amazing tools for interpreting the world. Some tools might make life easier. Other tools might make it more enjoyable. Extra senses could help people live longer, fuller lives.

FOCUS ON
EXTRA SENSES

Write your answers on a separate piece of paper.

1. Write a paragraph summarizing the main ideas from Chapter 1.

2. If you could gain an extra sense, what type would you want? Why?

3. Which extra sense has already been developed?

    A. a vest that can help deaf people sense sound
    B. a vest that monitors a person's vital signs
    C. a vest that gives the wearer 360-degree vision

4. Which of the following tasks could the BrainPort help a person do?

    A. listen to a concert
    B. navigate a busy street
    C. see heat through walls

Answer key on page 32.

GLOSSARY

artificial
Made by humans instead of occurring naturally.

engineers
People who design and create buildings or machines.

implant
A device that is placed inside the body by a surgeon.

interpret
To organize information in a way that gives meaning.

nerves
Long, thin fibers that carry information between the brain and other parts of the body.

organs
Sets of tissues that have specific jobs in the body.

perceive
To take in information through one of five natural senses.

plasticity
The quality of being easily shaped or changeable.

ultraviolet light
Light that is invisible to human eyes and has a shorter wavelength than that of visible light.

vibrate
To move back and forth quickly.

TO LEARN MORE

BOOKS

Bethea, Nikole Brooks. *Discover Bionics*. Minneapolis: Lerner Publications, 2017.

Loh-Hagan, Virginia. *Top 10: Super Senses*. Ann Arbor, MI: Cherry Lake Publishing, 2017.

Mattern, Joanne. *Super Senses*. South Egremont, MA: Red Chair Press, 2019.

NOTE TO EDUCATORS

Visit **www.focusreaders.com** to find lesson plans, activities, links, and other resources related to this title.

INDEX

Answer Key: **1.** Answers will vary; **2.** Answers will vary; **3.** A; **4.** B